Dedication:

To my dad, who sincerely raised us on the phrase, "You go girl!"

He cared for us in the best way possible— by teaching us how to grow our own wings, helping support us when we flapped those wings for the first time, and by giving us space and the freedom to fly.

Now that I have my own baby bird, I want her to know that there is no limit to what she can achieve with a goal, hard work, and faith.

Thank you also to these strong women who will help me teach her every day that if she can dream it, she can bring it to life InshAllah.

Prolance

www.prolancewriting.com
California, USA
©2021 Shazia Latif

ISBN: 978-1-7371558-2-9
Paperback edition

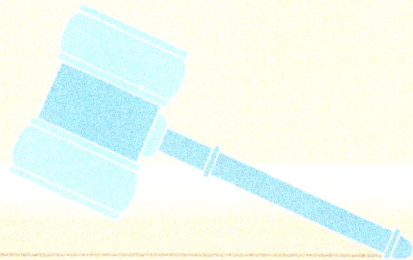

You Go Girl !

Naiya & 99 Muslim Female Trailblazers

Written by Shazia Latif
Illustrated by Palelee Puru

PROLANCE

Every night when Naiya's mom was tucking her into bed, she used to tell Naiya about a different woman who helped make the world a better place. These women used the talents that Allah gave them, worked hard, and always tried their best to help those around them. Their efforts went a long way towards shaping a world with more justice, beauty, and opportunity for all!

Women in Service!

Dr. Hawa Abdi

Dr. Hawa Abdi was a civil rights activist and a doctor. She offered free medical services to Somali women. Her small clinic grew into a huge hospital, and she helped patients during the Somali Civil War. She even opened a school for orphans and a relief camp which helped 90,000 people during a drought.

Shirin Ebadi

At age 22, Shirin Ebadi became the first female judge in Iran ever, and later became the first female judge to reach the status of Chief Justice. Shirin spent her career protecting the rights of women and children. She spoke out when she saw injustice happening in her country and fought to defend those who had no voice or power. She was awarded the Nobel Peace Prize for her defense of human rights and became the first Muslim woman to be awarded this prestigious prize!

ALFR·
NOBEL

Malala Yousafzai

When extremists tried to take away her right to go to school, Malala Yousafzai stood up and spoke out even though she was only 11 years old. Her safety was threatened but Malala continued to speak out for the rights of education for all children. In 2014 she became the youngest winner of the Nobel Peace Prize. Now she travels the world meeting with world leaders and working to improve education for all children around the world.

Atifete

Jahjaga

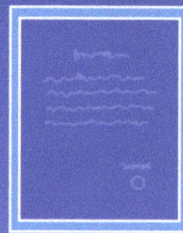

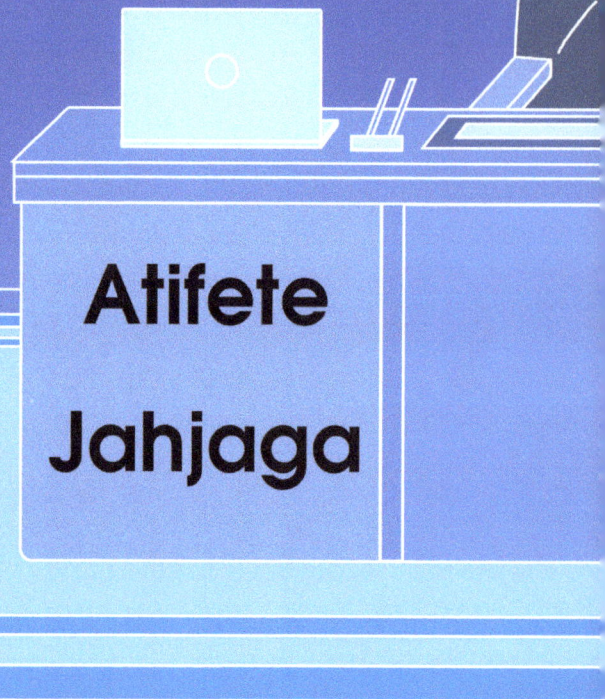

Atifete Jahjaga had an enormous responsibility as deputy director of the Kosovo police and a few years later, she earned an even greater responsibility as the first female president of Kosovo! Though she did not have a lot of political experience, Atifete was popular for her integrity and public service.

Atifete jahjaga

In her time as president, she focused on free speech, fair elections and encouraging more women and young people to have a voice in government. Atifete served her country with honor and trust.

Mame Madior Boye

Before she became the first female Prime Minister of Senegal, Mame Madior Boye was a lawyer who worked for justice in Senegal. She was highly respected for her honesty, intelligence and integrity. She served as the Minister of Justice before being appointed as Prime Minister. During her time in office, she worked to increase the number of women in government, strengthen education and health, reduce unemployment, and improve salaries for the people of Senegal!

Ameenah Gurib-Fakim

Ameenah Gurib-Fakim was the first woman elected as president of Mauritius. As president, she worked hard to make sure her nation could run itself without relying on help from other countries. Before becoming president, she was a celebrated scientist and professor. Her work highlighted the special plants that Mauritius has used for generations in treating illness and the animals that they needed to protect from extinction.

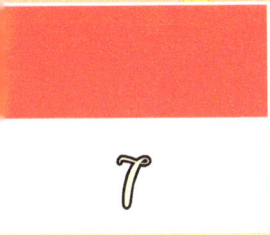

Cisse Sidibe

Growing up in Mali, Cisse Mariam Kaidama Sidibe had seen a lot of fighting over power in politics. She focused on establishing peace as a minister in Mali, because she knew that without peace, the country could not grow. After being appointed as the first female Prime Minister of Mali, she focused on helping her country move forward through education, specifically for women and girls. After her term, she continued to work for education, even partnering in a global effort to keep girls in school and improve literacy rates for women in developing nations.

Megawati Sukarnoputri

When your father is the president of the country, it seems natural that you might also be interested in politics but at first, Megawati Sukarnoputri of Indonesia was not. She studied agriculture and even ran a flower shop! She lived a regular life so many people in Indonesia connected with her as being just like them. She had a lot of popular support to get into politics though, so she did and she worked her way up to becoming the first female president of the country.

Tawakkol Karman

Tawakkol Karman is a woman who knows that standing up peacefully for what is right holds a great deal of power. As a journalist in Yemen, she saw a lot of other journalists getting in trouble for what they were writing and she led protests to make sure everyone was free to express themselves. She also works night and day to improve the rights and safety of women in her country. In 2011 she was awarded the Nobel Peace Prize for standing up for others, never giving up, and working peacefully to support rights for everyone in Yemen!

⑨

Azadeh N. Shahshahani

Having immigrated to the United States from Iran at a young age, Azadeh Shahshahani had first-hand experience of how challenging it can be to start life in a new country as an immigrant. She became a lawyer to defend the rights of immigrants and served as president of the National Lawyers Guild! She has even traveled to other countries to support human rights there through free elections and fair trials. She has helped countless immigrant communities and people with very little power to protect their rights.

Jamilah Nasheed

After losing both of her parents at a young age, Jamilah Nasheed was raised in extreme poverty in Missouri by her grandmother. Her life was headed down a troubled path until one day she received a pamphlet about Islam. She converted to Islam and although she never planned to go into politics, she decided to use her voice to help those without power in her community. She became the first Muslim woman to serve in a state legislature in the USA, serving a total of 5 terms, and worked with both Democrats and Republicans to do what was best for her community.

Saima Mohsin

When she first became a lawyer, Saima Mohsin worked for years as a federal prosecutor, making sure citizens in her area had equal access to justice. She served in the US Attorney's Office Violent and Organized Crime Unit, Drug Task Force, and General Crimes Unit. She worked her way up and became the first Muslim to be serving as US Attorney. As US Attorney, she is the highest law enforcement officer in her district, defending her community and keeping them safe from harm.

Zainab Salbi

Fleeing Iraq as a teenager, Zainab Salbi knew the agony of war and wanted to help others going through the same thing. At age 23, she created Women for Women International to help support women experiencing war in their countries.

In the first year she was able to help 33 women financially, emotionally, and with health services. Under Zainab's continued leadership, the organization grew and has helped almost 480,000 women!

Saadia Zahidi

14

When she was young growing up in Pakistan, Saadia Zahidi saw some women starting to work in careers that were usually dominated by men, like engineering and business. She saw how these role models were inspiring young girls to test out new careers. Now, Saadia creates plans for women to have awesome and exciting careers in developing countries!

Nana Asma'u

15

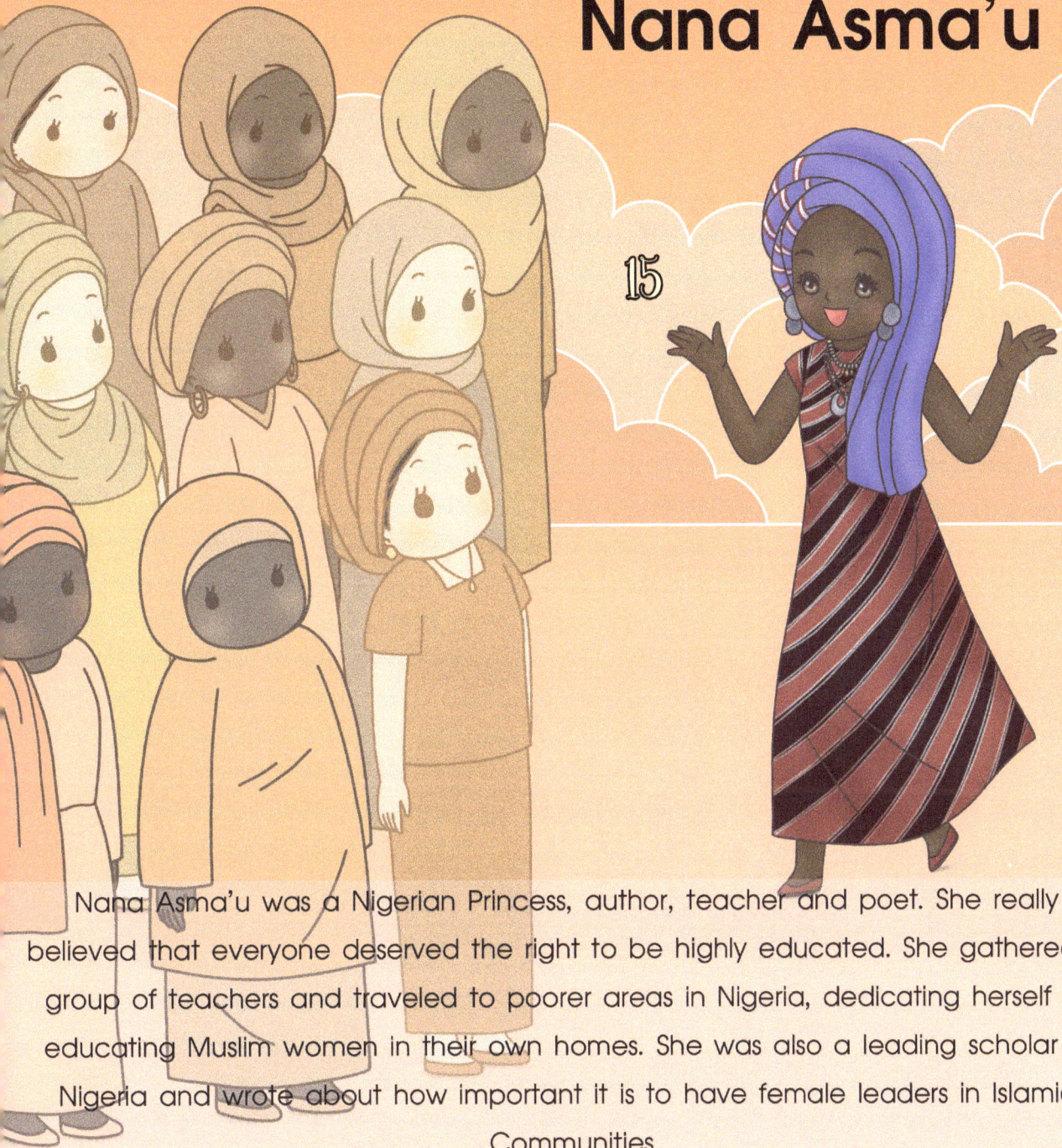

Nana Asma'u was a Nigerian Princess, author, teacher and poet. She really believed that everyone deserved the right to be highly educated. She gathered a group of teachers and traveled to poorer areas in Nigeria, dedicating herself to educating Muslim women in their own homes. She was also a leading scholar in Nigeria and wrote about how important it is to have female leaders in Islamic Communities.

Farah Pandith

Although she didn't start her career working in government, Farah Pandith wanted to show the true beauty of Islam on the world stage. She was appointed as the first-ever Special Representative to Muslim Communities by Hilary Clinton. Farah has worked with youth all over the world to create a network of young Muslims who want to have a positive impact in their communities. The organization has spread to over 30 countries and makes real changes every day in the lives of countless people, bringing light to the true spirit of Islam.

17

Dalia Mogahed

The largest and most comprehensive study of Muslims around the world was conducted by Dalia Mogahed. She interviewed over 50,000 Muslims in over 35 countries and her research took 6 years! She has been director of many research organizations, founded her own practice, and was selected as an advisor by President Obama! She co-wrote a book about the Muslim Community, our thoughts and opinions on a variety of topics and is considered a leading authority on statistics involving the Muslim community.

Queen Rania

When Rania Al-Abdullah married her prince, she became a princess but the fairy tale had just begun. Queen Rania has focused her time and influence to improve education, health, and overall well-being of all children.

She has championed the idea that every child is special and has something incredible to offer the world. Her work and her continued efforts have enabled a new generation of children to grow up with opportunity and potential to make the world a better place!

Women in the Arts!

Zaha Hadid

In an industry largely dominated by men, Zaha Hadid became one of the world's most famous architects. She designed large, soaring buildings in many different countries and was called the "Queen of the Curve" for the fluid style of her drawings.

She opened her own architecture firm, taught, and even designed shoes! She was also the first woman to receive the Pritzker Architecture Prize and the first woman ever to receive the Royal Institute of British Architects Gold Medal.

Nadiya Hussain

From home baker to baking the Queen's 90th birthday cake,
Nadiya Hussain's culinary adventure has been delicious and inspiring. After
winning the Great British Bake Off, she has hosted travel and cooking shows, written
cookbooks for adults and children, children's books, and a novel! She even designed
her own homeware collection and has become an ambassador for two charity
foundations. Nadiya has inspired a whole generation of home bakers to reach
for the stars!

Fatima Ali

Fatima Ali first learned to cook from her dad, her grandmother and their family's cook in Pakistan. She moved to America at 18 and became the youngest executive sous chef at a famous New York Restaurant. She's also famous for winning an episode of "Chopped" and being voted "fan favorite" for her sparkling personality on Top Chef!

Boushra Almutawakel

Boushra Almutawakel is the first professional female photographer
in Yemen. She uses her camera and her creativity to share
the many faces of Muslim women with the world and
has exhibited her work in many different countries!

Samira Ahmed

23

Being a high school English teacher for many years, Samira Ahmed recognized so much strength in her students and also saw how society could sometimes underestimate teenage power. In her New York Times bestselling novels, Samira writes vivid teenage Muslim characters who lead seemingly ordinary lives but summon their extraordinary inner power when circumstances call them to stand up for justice. So it was a perfect match when Samira became the first South Asian female to write a Ms. Marvel series centering around a Muslim American teenager who gains superhuman powers! Samira inspires her audience, Muslim and non-Muslim, to stand up for justice by engaging them through these incredible, dynamic, and extremely relatable characters.

Sukina Owen-Douglas

Harnessing the power of words is how Sukina Owen-Douglas shares her experiences, opinions, and creativity with the world. She is a spoken word poet and hip hop artist, and also works with women, children, and refugees, teaching the power of expression and healing through poetry.

24

When they noticed a lack of people who look like them in the hip hop and rap community, Sukina Owen-Douglas and Tanya Muneera Williams formed the duo Poetic Pilgrimage.

Tanya Muneera Williams

As an African-British Muslim rapper and advocate, Tanya Muneera Williams uses her voice and words to inspire women to have confidence in themselves. She hosts workshops to showcase stories from authors who normally do not have a platform due to their race, gender, or religion, with the goal to bring about education and social change.

25

Both women are talented poets and artists, and shatter the expectations of what a "Muslim Woman" does and what a "rapper" should look like. They use words and performance as their tools to open up a dialogue about female power and Islam.

Hana Tajima

At the end of the day, designer Hana Tajima wants all women to be free to be modest and still express themselves through fashion. She draws inspiration for her designs from her British-Japanese background, from her travels, and from nature. Islam inspires her dedication to respecting her body and all women through her designs. Making her fashionable hijabs and clothing available to women through a major international fashion label, Hana encourages women to be modest and still express themselves with their personal sense of style.

Yuna

27

As a teenager, Yuna taught herself how to play guitar and began writing her own songs. She has since become one of the most famous Malaysian singer-songwriters, was the first Malaysian singer to be nominated for a BET award, and has won multiple awards in Malaysia and the US for her work singing in both Malay and English. She also takes time to mentor other young singers and help them build their own music careers.

Halima Aden made a splash in the world of fashion as the first contestant to wear hijab in the Miss Minnesota pageant. She was also the first hijab-wearing model to walk international runways and to be signed with one of the largest modeling agencies in the world! Huge fashion labels have supported Halima's decision to wear hijab and have tailored their fashion to fit her preference for modesty. She has proven that women don't need to compromise their values to be successful in fashion!

28

Halima Aden

One message that hijabi model Mariah Idrissi would like you to know is that you can achieve anything you aim for by being yourself- you don't need to conform or compromise your beliefs. As a young model, Mariah took part in a campaign for an international fashion brand and captured attention for being the first hijabi model to represent an international brand. From the beginning, she made it very clear that she would make high fashion work for her- not the other way around.

29
Mariah Idrissi

Lena Khan

When Lena Khan started making movies, she hardly saw anyone who looked like her in Hollywood. At times she felt doubts that anyone would want to hear her stories, but soon realized that her unique identity and perspective were to her benefit in the industry. Her first feature film was the story of her parents' immigrant experience and she has since directed a movie for Disney! Her main goal is to use film as an entertaining way to call attention to important issues.

DIRECTOR

30

BREAKING NEWS

Amna Nawaz

When Amna Nawaz started studying journalism, she fell in love with the process-searching for information, seeing the impact of a well-done story, and learning something new every day! She worked as a TV anchorwoman, a foreign correspondent, and delivered breaking news coverage.

One of her highest moments in journalism was being the first Muslim to moderate a Presidential Debate!

Negin Farsad 32

As a "social justice comedian," Negin Farsad realized that she could make a huge difference in the world just by making people laugh. Balancing multiple projects as a comedian, actress, writer, and filmmaker, Negin has made it her mission to mix her creativity with important messages that will help open peoples' minds and hearts. She has written a musical, made a feature film, written a book, and started her own production company! She sees laughter as a way to connect people from all backgrounds.

Faiza Saleem 33

As Pakistan's first social media entertainer, Faiza Saleem has posted comedy skits all over the internet, working to change the typical way women are shown in media. Comedy in Pakistan has been very male-dominated but Faiza is working to change that, organizing the first female comedy group in Pakistan.

Maysoon Zayid 34

While pursuing a career as a stand up comedian, there was only one little thing that Maysoon Zayid found difficult- standing! Maysoon lives with Cerebral Palsy - a condition that impacts balance, posture and movements - but did that stop her from chasing her dreams? No way! Maysoon has performed her comedy all over the United States, in the Arab world, and co-founded the New York Arab American Comedy Festival. She has also acted in TV and movies, and wants to continue working in media to increase the visibility of people with disabilities.

She is also working to mentor a new generation of female comedians. Through her comedy Faiza also celebrates the idea of body positivity in Pakistan. She has even modeled plus size clothing in Pakistan, working to show that women of all sizes have a place in the spotlight.

Zarqa Nawaz

Zarqa Nawaz originally went to school for journalism, but used her story-telling skills in a lot of different ways. She created the world's first sitcom about a Muslim community in the west called Little Mosque on the Prairie. It became famous internationally, boasted the highest ratings on the network, and won multiple awards! She is also an author, speaker, journalist, broadcaster, producer, stand-up comedian, and recently began her own web series!

Waad Al-Kateab

For 5 years, journalist and filmmaker Waad Al-Kateab recorded her life in Syria during their civil war. After she and her family were forced to leave Syria for their safety, she edited over 500 hours of her footage into a documentary to bring awareness to the world about what is really happening in Syria. Waad's documentary won the BAFTA Award for Best Documentary and set a record for the most nominations. She also won Best Documentary at the Cannes Film Festival and was named one of Time Magazine's Most Influential People. Waad sees filmmaking as her way to stand up for justice and hopes to bring light to the situation in Syria, especially for the family and friends who she had to leave behind.

Rawdah Mohamed

After being forced to leave Somalia during the civil war and spending many years in a refugee camp in Kenya, Rawdah Mohamed's family moved to Norway when she was 9. Visibly Muslim and having darker skin than her Norweigan classmates, Rawdah was often bullied but that only strengthened her resolve to stand up for others. As an adult, she was initially noticed on social media for her modest street fashion but used her popularity to stand up for the rights of French Muslim women to wear their hijab in public. When Rawdah was named fashion editor of Vogue Scandinavia, she became the first hijab-wearing editor of color for a western fashion magazine!

Women in Science and Technology!

Dr. Burcin Matlu-Pakdil

When she was young, Burcin Matlu-Pakdil loved to
look into the night sky. Little did she know then that
when she got older, she would become a prominent
astrophysicist and astronomer, and even discover
an extremely rare new galaxy! It was nicknamed
"Burcin's Galaxy" and is a huge scientific breakthrough!
Now she co-chairs a Women in Astronomy group and
wants to inspire more Muslim women to follow their
dreams, and enter the field of science without hesitation.

Anousheh Anşari

Can you imagine seeing the Earth from outer space?! In 2006, Anousheh Ansari became the first female Muslim to do so! Back on Earth, she co-founded a technology company, and has won many awards for her success in business and technology. Anousheh hopes to inspire young Muslim girls to keep their eyes on their dreams, even if they seem out of this world, and to reach for the stars!

Dr. Tahani Amer

Helping her dad fix his car when she was young was "outside the box" for a young girl in Egypt. But to Dr. Tahani Amer, she was learning about how machines work, which is what she has always loved to do. She went on to get her doctorate in engineering, started working for NASA, and even invented a new system for NASA! She also mentors young students because she always wants to give back to other young people who love thinking outside of the box.

Dr. Ismahane Elouafi

When becoming a fighter pilot was no longer her dream job, Dr. Ismahane Elouafi earned her PhD in genetics instead. She researched crops that are usually forgotten about and tested them in areas that do not have successful food sources. She also studied farming that does not require fresh water, and her innovative work has helped feed many people in Asia, Africa, and the Middle East!

41

42

Dr. Katijah Yousoff

Dr. Katijah Yousoff has always believed in using science to create real solutions for people around the world. She is famous for her research on the Newcastle Disease Virus –a disease that causes deadly infections in birds– and her work has expanded to potentially help in the treatment of certain cancers! Her research and influence helped develop policies to further science in Malaysia, helped poor farmers in Africa, and have inspired many other young scientists to carry on her work.

43

TRUE NEWS

Dr. Sameena Shah is an engineer who combines her love of technology and problem-solving to help other industries grow. Her motivation is her curiosity and her expertise is in designing Artificial Intelligence.

Dr. Sameena Shah

FALSE NEWS

One of her top accomplishments was to design a program for a major news organization to sift false news from true news online, enabeling them to report their news more accurately.

Dr. Hayat bint Sulaiman bin Hassan Sindi

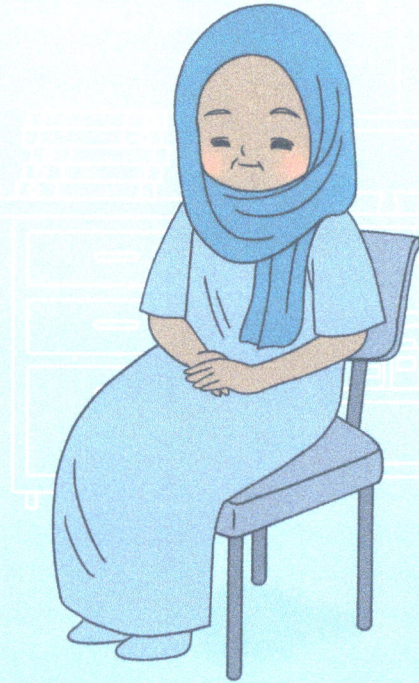

As a medical scientist, Dr. Hayat Sindi used her expertise in biotechnology to rethink how doctors can help their patients more during their time together. She was the first woman from the entire Arab States of the Persian Gulf to complete a doctoral degree in biotechnology and was one of the first women to join the Consultative Assembly of Saudi Arabia. Her mission has centered around helping people using simple and affordable solutions, and encouraging science education especially for women in the Middle East.

Dr. Maryam Matar

Thanks to the work of Dr. Maryam Matar, a whole new generation of healthier children are being born in the United Arab Emirates. She devoted her research to studying genetic diseases, single-handedly putting the UAE on the map for genetic research, and created an association to teach young families about genetic diseases. Because of her persistence to change hearts and minds, several laws have been passed to give families access to genetic screening. She is also the first woman Director-General of the Dubai Health Authority and the first woman to be Undersecretary of Public Health and Primary Healthcare in the history of the UAE!

Dr. Rim Turkmani

Dr. Rim Turkmani has always been curious about the world around her and lets her curiosity be her guide. She was already an accomplished astrophysicist in Europe when she saw that the civil war in her home country of Syria made it impossible for kids there to get to school. She was curious about how to solve the issue, so she followed her curiosity trying to create solutions. She now heads two major research programs studying how to transition from war to peace in Syria, and is part of a UN committee to help bring education to those in need.

46

Aisha Elsafty

In a disaster area, wireless technology can be a saving grace for people to communicate with loved ones and let them know that they are ok or that they need help. Computer scientist Aisha Elsafty's "AdHoc Networking" makes it possible for computers, phones, and other wireless technology to function during disasters and in developing areas. Her work allows families to keep in touch even under the most challenging circumstances.

Dr. Adawia Alousi

48

Dr. Adawia Alousi was a pioneer in the field of science, developing a treatment for heart failure and creating a new medicine to make the heart beat stronger. It was uncommon at her time for a woman to go into high-level science and so education was something that she held very close to her heart throughout her life. After passing away, Adawia's estate has helped pay for many young Muslim women, especially refugees and immigrants, to have the opportunity to join STEM programs to make their own positive impact on the world.

Dr. Khawla Al-Kuraya

49

Dr. Khawla Al-Kuraya is a doctor and scientist specializing in cancer research and pathology- the study of the causes and effects of diseases. She was the first to identify a gene in the human body that forms cancer cells and was the first Saudi woman to receive the "Order of Abdulaziz al Saud" for her work in cancer research.

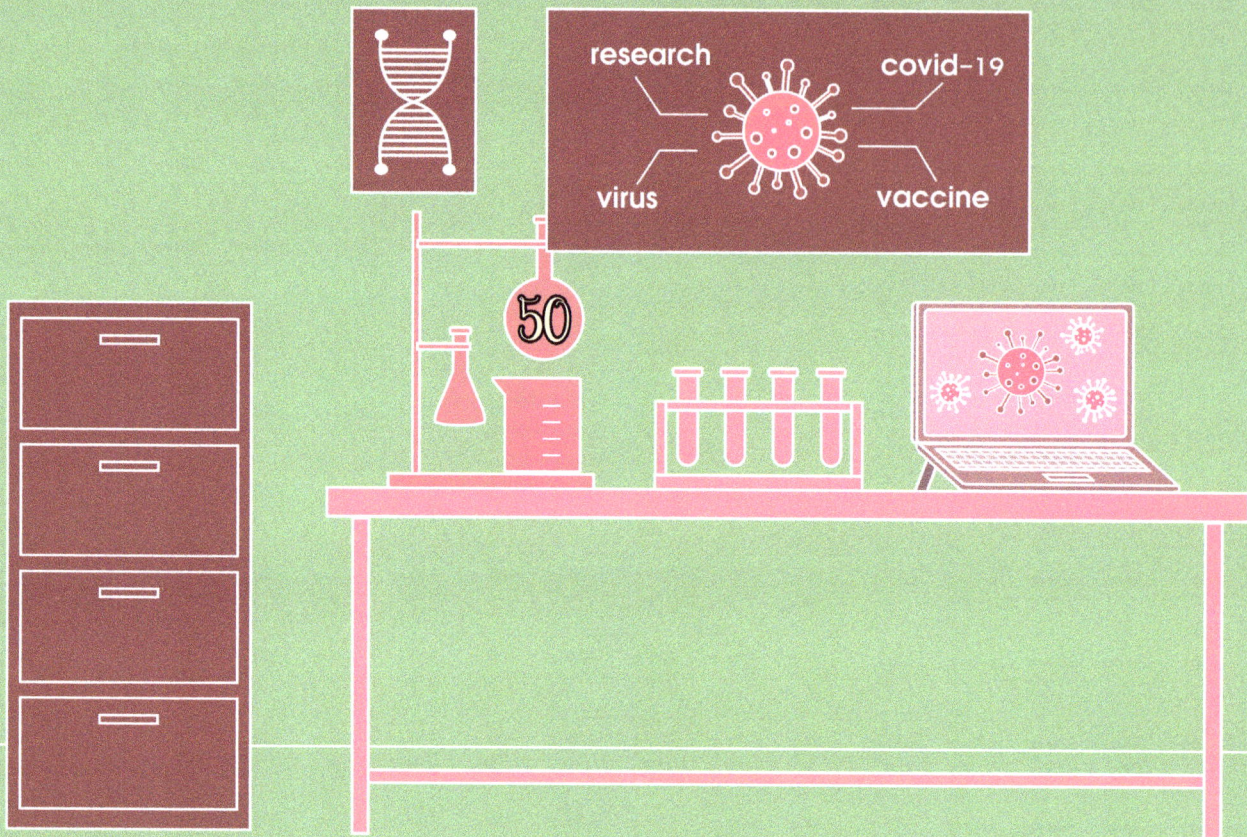

When the COVID-19 Pandemic plunged the entire world into uncertainty, Dr. Ozlem Tureci and her husband changed the course of their research, from finding a cure for cancer towards finding a vaccine for the virus. Prior to this, she had established two very successful biotech companies and had discovered a way to use the body's own immune system to treat cancer! In 2020 however, she and her husband led their team towards a new kind of cure, becoming the first in the world to achieve a 90% efficacy rating.

Dr. Ozlem Tureci

Women in Sports!

Kulsoom Abdullah

Kulsoom Abdullah changed the history of competitive weightlifting when she was denied the right to compete because her arms and legs were covered. The International Weightlifting Federation (IWF) had this rule because judges needed to see when the elbows and knees of competitors "locked" to judge the success of a lift. Pressure was put on the IWF to allow her to compete while wearing modest clothing, including her hijab, and the IWF agreed as long as they could clearly make calls about her lifts. Kulsoom went on to become the first female weightlifter to represent Pakistan at the World Championships and was also the first female to compete while wearing hijab, with full coverage of her arms and legs. Thanks to Kulsoom's strength, other sports leagues around the world began allowing athletes to wear modest clothing as part of their rules, which opened up opportunities for other Muslim women to compete in sports that had once been out of their reach.

Ines Boubakri

When she was a girl, Ines Boubakri looked up to her mom as a fencer and began training with her mother as her coach. With hard work and motivation, she is now Africa's highest ranked women's foil fencer! She is 13-time African National Champion and won the bronze medal at the 2016 Olympics. She is the first Tunisian fencer ever to win an Olympic medal and the 1st African woman to win a fencing medal.

Ibtihaj Muhammad

53

Ibtihaj Muhammad was always athletic, but chose fencing as her main sport because the uniform was more modest. When people would tell her that there was no place for her in fencing, it actually motivated her to push harder. In 2016, Ibtihaj made history as the 1st female Muslim American athlete to earn a medal at the Olympics, she was the 1st US woman to wear hijab while competing at the Olympics, and is 5-time Senior World Champion! She even had a Barbie modeled after her, which was the first hijabi and first fencing Barbie ever.

Farkhondeh Sadegh & Laleh Keshavarz

In 2005, Farkhondeh Sadegh, a graphic designer, and Laleh Keshavarz, a dentist, made history as the first Muslim women to climb Mount Everest! They faced major climbing dangers such as avalanches, falling into valleys, low oxygen, and extremely bad weather. However, both ladies were motivated to keep climbing because they felt that their achievement would highlight the potential for other Muslim women in sports. It took 10 weeks, but Farkhondeh and Laleh celebrated as they reached the summit and cemented their place in history!

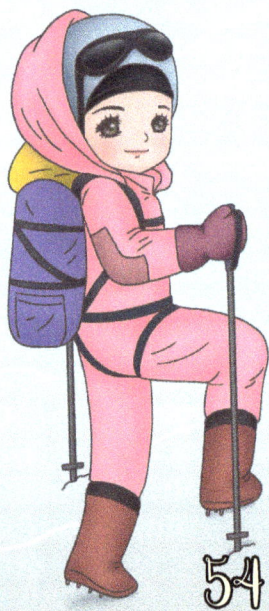

55

56

Manal Rostom

When she started in the world of marathons and mountaineering, Manal Rostom found that she did not have many hijabi Muslim women to look up to. Sometimes she would be given a hard time for competing in hijab, but she never let that stop her. She is now the first Egyptian to have completed 5 of the 6 world marathon majors and has scaled 2 of the world's highest mountains! She is also the first hijab-wearing athlete to appear in a Nike Middle East Campaign and became the global face of the Nike Pro Hijab in 2017.

54

Samina Baig

When she was young, Samina Baig's uncles, dad, and brothers were all mountain climbers and used to tell her about their adventures when they returned from an expedition. Samina wanted to climb but in Pakistan, mountaineering is not a typical sport for a female. Samina broke all kinds of barriers when she became the first Pakistani woman to climb Mount Everest and was the youngest Muslim woman to do so at age 21! After scaling Peak Chaskin Sar in Pakistan it was nicknamed "Samina Peak" and she is also the first Muslim to climb all 7 major summits in the world!

57

Faranak Partoazar

From an early age in Iran, Faranak Partoazar loved adventure but when she started riding a bike for fun, it was not widely accepted. Sometimes the authorities would even stop her and take her to the police station for breaking traditions! She fought and became a professional mountain biker, competing as part of Iran's National Team. She has won every national title and race in Iran, was the 1st female Iranian cyclist to win a medal at the Asian Championships, and she is ranked as the #1 female Asian rider.

58

Fatmire Alushi

At age 5, Fatmire Alushi had to leave her home in Kosovo as a refugee and move with her family to Germany. She used to play soccer with her brothers as a way to prove herself to the new kids around her and she kept getting better and better. She signed her first professional contract at age 16, was part of the World Cup winning team in 2007, was one of Nike's featured athletes, and became one of the highest paid players in Europe! Fatmire is a proud Muslim woman and sees her religion as a source of pride.

Nadia Nadim

When her family was forced to flee Afghanistan, Nadia Nadim did not know that this tragedy would later lead her into triumph. It was in a refugee camp in Denmark that Nadia began playing soccer as a way to be a regular kid and to integrate into Danish society. She became the first foreign-born player to play for the Danish National Team while she was also taking her exams to become a surgeon! Nadia used her early experiences to fuel her passions and now she works with other refugees to show them that no matter what they have been though, they can achieve their dreams too.

Bilqis Abdul-Qaadir

Bilqis Abdul-Qaadir started playing basketball at 4 and by the time she was in high school, she had broken both the male and female scoring records in Massachusetts! She became the first female player in NCAA history to play while wearing hijab and was named Gatorade Player of the Year. When she wanted to go on playing professionally in Europe however, she encountered a road block – international basketball had a rule against head coverings. Bilqis really believed in dressing modestly, even on the court, but had to choose- her faith or her athletic career. She chose to stick with her faith, and instead started an online campaign to raise awareness for Muslim women in sports. When the ban on headscarves was eventually lifted, Bilqis was invited to play for multiple teams. However she declined and wants to continue working to advocate for other girls so that they never have to choose between their faith and their athletic passions.

Indira Kaljo

Coming to America from Bosnia at a young age, Indira Kaljo fell in love with basketball and was a really successful player. When she decided to put on hijab in her 20s, she found that she was no longer able to play in international tournaments because of a ban on head coverings, which included her hijab. She started an online campaign to get the ban lifted, and got 70,000 signatures of support! The International Basketball Federation changed its rules to allow head coverings, making space for many women of faith to take center stage on the court.

62

Sifan Hassan

Leaving her birth country of Ethiopia as a refugee at age 15, Sifan Hassan arrived in the Netherlands and began running while studying to become a nurse. She excelled and became the World Champion for the 1500m run in 2016. She went on to win 2 gold medals at the 2019 World Championships (in the 1500m and 10,000m runs) and is the only athlete (male or female) to ever win both events at a single World Champion or Olympic Games. She is also the world record holder for the 5km road race and the mile, as well as the 1 hour run.

63

Rahaf Khatib

Only a few years after she began running recreationally, Rahaf Khatib made history as the first hijabi to appear on the cover of a fitness magazine in 2016. She has been busy co-creating the Adidas Hijab, running marathons, and coaching "Girls on the Run" which is an initiative to inspire hijabi women to get active and stay healthy. Her major motivation as a mom is to show her kids that with hard work and persistence, they can achieve anything!

Maryam Yusuf Jamal

In her career as a middle distance runner, Maryam Yusuf Jamal has made history multiple times. Primarily, she is the first Bahraini athlete ever to win an Olympic medal. Her gold medal at the 2012 Olympics also landed her a place in history as the first Olympic medal won by a woman representing the Gulf States. She is also the 2x World Champion in the 1500m race!

64

65

Dalilah Muhammad

From the time she was young, Dalilah Muhammad loved being on the track. As she got older though, she noticed that talent alone wasn't enough- she was going to need to train very hard to achieve her goals. She didn't qualify for the Olympics in 2012 but pushed herself to work even harder and qualified in 2016! Dalilah won a gold medal for the 400m hurdles that year and in 2019, she won another gold medal at the World Championships, setting a world record time for the 400m hurdles!

66

67

Khadijah Diggs

Khadijah Diggs's first triathlon was actually an initiation for her sorority but she fell in love and continued entering races. To date, she has entered more than 40 events and is ranked in the top 5% of her age group for the Ironman Triathlon. She is also the first Muslim woman to represent Team USA in a multisport event and the first African American woman to represent Team USA in the Long Course Triathlon. Her main goal is to make her family proud and to promote a positive image of Islam, and especially Muslim women, through sports!

Sania Mirza

Society did not encourage girls to play sports professionally when Sania Mirza was young in India, but she decided to go for it anyway. She started playing tennis and has become one of the highest paid and most high profile athletes in India! She has won 6 Grand Slam Titles, was ranked India's #1 player for 10 years and has won 14 medals! She even established her own tennis academy, and was the first South Asian Woman to be appointed as a Goodwill Ambassador!

Dinara Safina

Dinara Safina grew up in a tennis family- her dad directed a tennis club in Moscow, her mom coached tennis, and her brother was a professional tennis player. However, they never pressured Dinara to play. When she decided she wanted to join her family legacy, her mom coached her. Dinara won the silver medal at the 2008 Summer Olympics and was ranked #1 in the world in 2009! Unfortunately, a major back injury forced her to retire from professional tennis but now she is a tennis coach for other young rising tennis players.

Aliya Mustafina

After earning many titles, Aliya Mustafina is considered one of the most successful female artistic gymnasts of all time! She is the 2010 All-Around World Champion, 2013 European All-Around World Champion, 2012 and 2016 uneven bars champion and is a 7 time Olympic medalist! She operates under the mindset that she doesn't need to prove anything to anyone else- she works hard to prove to herself that she can do what she sets her mind to.

Doaa Elghobashy & Nada Meawad

71

72

70

Doaa Elghobashy and Nada Meawad made history at their first Olympic Games as the youngest competitors in Olympic Women's Beach Volleyball. (Doaa was 19 and Nada was 18). They also made history as Egypt's first ever Olympic team to compete in beach volleyball. People were impressed by their athletic talent especially considering their uniforms- rather than wearing bathing suits as per usual in the sport, Doaa and Nada opted to wear more modest long pants and shirts. Doaa also wore a hijab, which made her the first hijabi in Olympic Beach Volleyball history!

Bianca "Bam Bam" Elmir

When she was growing up, a lot of things were out of Bianca Elmir's control. Her parents divorced when she was very young, and she lived between their two households in Australia and Lebanon. Faith and sports gave Bianca stability and her confidence as an athlete turned into self-confidence in real life. She has earned the titles of Australian Flyweight Champion and Oceania Boxing Bantamweight Champion.

Ruqsana Begum

Standing at just over 5' tall, the first word you would use to describe Ruqsana Begum would probably not be "fighter". However, she is a professional kickboxer, boxer, and Muay Thai fighter! She was nominated to be captain of the British Muay Thai team, she has won the British Muay Thai Atomweight Kickboxing Champion Professional Title, and won the gold medal at the European Club Cup Amateur Muay Thai Championship. In fact, Ruqsana is the only Muslim woman who is a national champion in her sport!

Zhazira Zhapparkul

75

Zhazira Zhapparkul is a Kazakh Olympian weightlifter. She won silver medals at both the 2014 and 2015 World Championships and when she represented Kazakhstan at the 2016 Olympics she won a silver medal!

Sri Wahyuni Agustiani

Sri Wahyuni Agustiani is an Indonesian Weightlifter, who has taken home 4 silver medals at major weightlifting competitions: the 2013 Asian Championships, the 2014 Asian Games, the 2016 Olympics, and the 2018 Asian Games!

76

Sara Ahmed

With a father and brother who are both national competitive weightlifters, it's no wonder that Sara Ahmed's family encouraged her to get involved in sports! She went on to win the bronze medal for weightlifting at the 2016 Olympics. Sara has set a lot of records in her career, being named the "Best Female Lifter" at the Junior World Championships, becoming the first Arab Woman to receive an Olympic weightlifting medal, and the first Egyptian woman to receive an Olympic medal in any discipline!

Zahra Lari

78

At age 11, Zahra Lari watched a Disney Movie about figure skating and decided that is what she wanted to do with her life. She trained really diligently and became the first person from the United Arab Emirates to compete internationally. She was also the first to compete in a hijab and is a 5-time Emirati National Champ! Additionally, she was instrumental in getting hijab recognized as an official piece of her skating costume!

Alina Zagitova

When she began skating at age 4, Alina Zagitova had no idea that by 18, she would be ranked one of the top 10 female figure skaters in the world! Alina had to sacrifice a lot to achieve her goals, even moving away from her parents to work with a professional coach, but it all paid off. Alina has broken 5 world records, won multiple gold medals, and was named Athlete of the Year in her home country of Russia!

Kubra Dagli

At age 13, Kubra Dagli started training in taekwondo. Waking up early and training daily for competitions became her routine and in 2016 it all paid off when she won the gold medal in the World Taekwondo Championship! Many people were so astonished that a woman wearing hijab won the award, but Kubra knew it was her hard work, motivation and talent that helped her achieve her dreams.

Hedaya Malak

Hedaya Malak started wrestling at age 6, wanting to be just like her older brother. In 2016 she won the bronze medal for featherweight taekwondo at the Olympics and became the 1st woman to win an Olympic medal in taekwondo for Egypt.

Nur Tatar

Nur Tatar won her first taekwondo medal at age 15. She has since won the silver medal in middleweight at the 2012 Olympics, bronze medal in welterweight at the 2016 Olympics, and has earned the titles for the Turkish Taekwondo World Champion and European Champion.

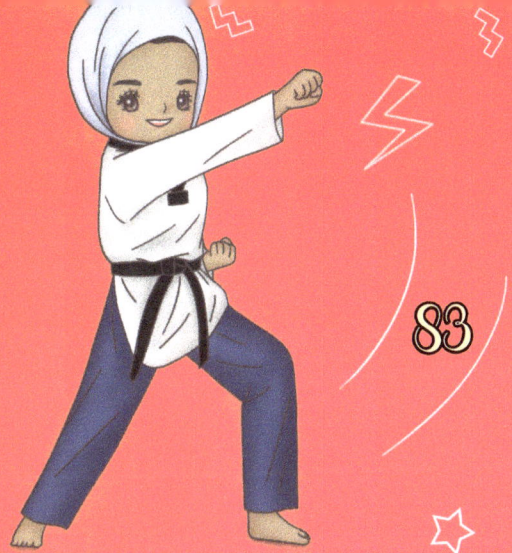

Kimia Al-Zadeh Zanouzi

Kimia became the first Iranian woman to win an Olympic medal when she took home bronze for featherweight taekwondo in 2016.

Patimat Abakarova

Patimat Abakarova won a bronze medal in flyweight taekwondo at the 2016 Olympics representing Azerbaijan.

Majlinda Kelmendi

Because Kosovo was not officially recognized by the International Olympics Committee until 2014, many athletes from Kosovo competed on behalf of other countries up to that time. When Kosovo was recognized, its athletes knew they needed to prove themselves on the world stage. In 2016, Majlinda Kelmendi became the first athlete from Kosovo to win an Olympic medal when she competed in judo. With her gold, she not only made history but also inspired a generation of young people in Kosovo to reach for dreams that seemed impossible before.

Mariya Stadnik

Mariya Stadnik is a three time Olympic medalist for female wrestling and was named the "Best Woman Wrestler on the Planet" by the International Wrestling Federation. She is also the youngest sportswoman in history to win an Olympic medal for Azerbaijan.

Marwa Amin

When Marwa Amin was 9, her father passed away. At age 12, she began wrestling which was highly unusual for a girl in Tunisia at the time. However, she put her heart and soul into it and won the bronze medal at the 2016 Olympics. She became the 1st woman from Africa to win an Olympic medal in wrestling.

Khadijah Mellah

At age 18, Khadijah Mellah not only became the first hijabi jockey in a British competitive horse race, but she was the the first British Muslim to win a competitive horse race! In the lead up to the race, there were many obstacles in her path- she was busy studying for exams while she trained, she trained during Ramadan, she was the youngest rider in the race and by far the least experienced. With all of that stacked against her, she still won the Magnolia Cup! There was a documentary made about her journey and she was awarded The Times' Young Sportswoman of the Year!

Noor Ahmed

89

Even though she didn't enjoy golf at first, Noor Ahmed stuck with it and started enjoying seeing herself improve in the game. When she earned an athletic and academic scholarship for college, she encountered a lot of people who had never met a Muslim before, even on her golf team. But when they got to know her, it really opened their minds as to what it means to be Muslim. Everyday on the green, Noor feels confident in breaking stereotypes as the first Division 1 golfer to wear a hijab and also as a woman in a typically male dominated sport.

Stephanie Kurlow

When she was 9 years old, Stephanie Kurlow's choice to wear a hijab was not typical in the world of ballet and so she was rejected from many ballet companies. Her mother saw how difficult this was for Stephanie and decided to help by opening her own ballet studio (go mom!). Stephanie was able to pursue her dreams and became the world's first hijabi ballerina! What initially set her apart has now become a strength for her and her story has earned her scholarships for dance as well as the spot as a face of many fashion brands!

90

Amar Hadid

Amar Hadid is an Australian skateboarder who earned the world's first University Skateboarding Scholarship! She is an Elite Athlete and has her sights set on representing Australia in the Olympics. She has also been selected twice as an Australia Day Ambassador and is studying medicine! As a proud Muslim, philanthropy motivated her to organize "World Tribute Day" as a global tribute to essential and healthcare workers, as well as victims of Covid-19.

Amna Al Qubaisi

Inspired by her dad who is a celebrated competitive driver, Amna Al Qubaisi began karting at age 14. Her dad coached her and now Amna has made history in multiple ways, as the 1st Emirati female race car driver, the 1st Arab female to win the UAE RMC Championship and the first female to take part in the GCC Young Drivers Academy Programme (which she won). She is also the 1st Arab female to win in a single seater category and the first female to be sponsored by Kaspersky Lab!

Aries Susanti Rahayu

93

Speed climbing is traditionally dominated by men but Aries Susanti Rahayu loves a challenge. She started by climbing trees as a girl and her talents increased as she got older. She has won multiple gold medals for speed climbing and in 2019 she broke the world record for women's speed climbing, even though she had a hand injury at the time! She has been nicknamed "spider woman" and says she is always looking ahead to see how she can continue to grow as a climber.

Shabnim Ismail

When she was young, Shabnim Ismail played cricket but almost quit because she would get so frustrated when she would strike out. Her coach convinced her to try bowling (pitching) instead and that was when the magic happened! Although she is shorter, Shabnim has become one of the fastest bowlers in women's cricket. She is the only Muslim woman to have played international cricket for South Africa and in a male dominated sport, Shabnim has made history as the first South African (male or female) to win "Player of the Match" in the finals of the Big Bash League!

Women in Business!

MALALA FUND

As a teenager in Pakistan, Shiza Shahid volunteered at a prison and in a relief camp for earthquake victims. She felt that every girl in Pakistan should be educated, and when she went to college at Stanford she felt even stronger about introducing educational opportunities for girls back home.

Shiza Shahid

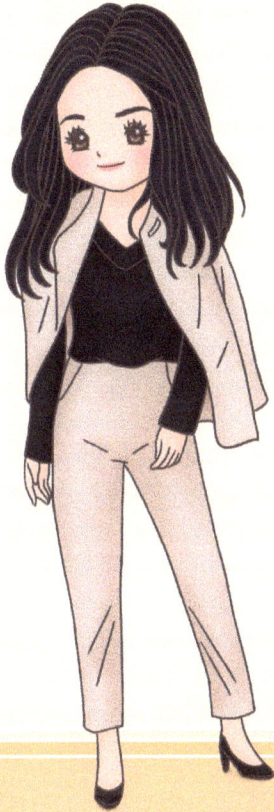

Over summer break back in Pakistan, Shiza created a girls summer camp to spark their love of learning and one of those girls was Malala Yousufzai. Later, Shiza helped Malala's family when she was hurt, and eventually established the Malala Fund, which promotes education for every girl.

Nora Al Shaaban

Traditionally in Saudi Arabia, women had not been encouraged to look for careers outside the home. However, this trend has been changing and women like Nora Al Shaaban have been at the forefront. She is an educator and a business woman. She has trained thousands of people in the Middle East, Europe and Asia in important business skills such as youth leadership, public speaking, and communication.

96

Nora Al Shaaban

Additionally, she is a chief executive of a company which encourages more women to join the workforce and promotes creative opportunities for women.

Vivy Yusof

Vivy Yusof originally went to school for law but started an online platform when she was 23 to bring multiple modest fashion and beauty brands under one roof. Little did she know that it would grow into a multimillion dollar company!

Next, she started her own really successful fashion brand to celebrate women wearing scarves, whether they were Muslim or not. She has won several business awards and works with a global organization to mentor other young entrepreneurs.

Nancy Hoque

Nancy Hoque already had a successful career designing communication systems for the military and first responders when she decided to take her career in a new direction.

Nancy wears a scarf and always saw hijab as a display of power and style for women. As a side project, she started a scarf company and within 6 months she was selling her scarves in 20 countries! Nancy is a global advocate for women to take and create their own positions of leadership.

Melanie Elturk

As a young girl, Melanie Elturk wanted to feel beautiful wearing her hijab, but noticed that there was a lack of fashionable, modest clothing options on the market. She found creative ways to incorporate her love of fashion into her modest clothing choices, and eventually made a business out of it!

She is founder and CEO of one of the largest American Hijab brands and takes her mission of making Muslim women feel confident everyday very seriously. For her, clothing choices go beyond simple fashion- it is a way to express your devotion to Allah while maintaining your personal style and expressing yourself!

After learning about all of these amazing women and the ways they used their talents to help others, Naiya couldn't wait to jump out of bed ready to start a new day!

When she was ready to leave for school, Naiya's mom kissed her on the cheek and said, "The world is a better place because you are here. I know you can make a difference too!"

Her mom always
believed that Naiya
had the power and
talent to change the
world.

And so do you!

Author's note:
The women in this book have worked hard and achieved amazing accomplishments in their professional careers. They are the first and/ or best in their fields and that is why we are celebrating their work in this book.

www.ingramcontent.com/pod-product-compliance
Lightning Source LLC
Chambersburg PA
CBHW050257090426
42734CB00023B/3488